Meal Prep Ketogenic Cookbook

Beginners Meal Prep Guide With 70 Ketogenic Diet Recipes And 2 Week Meal Plan For Quicker Weight Loss

NANCY CREWS

Copyright © 2017 Nancy Crews

All rights reserved. No part of this publication may be reproduced, distributed, or transmitted in any form or by any means, including photocopying, recording, or other electronic or mechanical methods, without the prior written permission of the publisher, except in the case of brief quotations embodied in critical reviews and certain other noncommercial uses permitted by copyright law.

Limit of Liability/Disclaimer of Warranty: While the publisher and author have used their best efforts in preparing this book, they make no representations or warranties with respect to the accuracy or completeness of the contents of this book and specifically disclaim any implied warranties of merchantability or fitness for a particular purpose. No warranty may be created or extended by sales representatives or written sales materials. The advice and strategies contained herein may not be suitable for your situation. You should consult with a professional where appropriate. Neither the publisher nor author shall be liable for any loss of profit or any other commercial damages, including but not limited to special, incidental, consequential, or other damages.

ISBN-13: 978-1976340291
ISBN-10: 1976340292

DEDICATION

To all who desire to live life to the fullest!

TABLE OF CONTENT

Read Other Books By Nancy Crews: ix
INTRODUCTION 1
    Meal Prep Benefits 2
    Meal Prep Beginners' Guide 3
    Tips For Making Meal Prep Easy 6
2 WEEK MEAL PLAN 9
    Week 1, Day 1 9
    Week 1, Day 2 9
    Week 1, Day 3 10
    Week 1, Day 4 11
    Week 1, Day 5 11
    Week 1, Day 6 12
    Week 1, Day 7 13
    Week 2, Day 1 13
    Week 2, Day 2 14
    Week 2, Day 3 15
    Week 2, Day 4 15
    Week 2, Day 5 16
    Week 2, Day 6 17
    Week 2, Day 7 17
BREAKFAST 19
    Egg, Bacon And Cheese Cups 20
    Omelet Roll 21

Vanilla Smoothie 23

Zucchini And Walnut Bread 24

Ricotta Blueberry Pancakes 25

Breakfast Sausage Casserole 27

Lemon Poppyseed Muffins 29

White Pizza Frittata 31

Quiche With Almond Crust 32

Creamy Cheese Pancakes 34

Feta, Spinach And Sausage Frittata 35

Chocolate Smoothie 37

No-Flour Waffles 38

Overnight Flaxseed Meal 39

Cauliflower Herbed Egg Muffins 40

Breakfast Egg Muffins 42

Brownie Muffins 43

Pumpkin Pancakes 45

Chicken Omelet 46

Homemade Patties 47

LUNCH 49

Spicy Chili 50

Chicken Salad 52

Chili Con Carne 53

Chicken And Cauliflower Casserole 55

Chicken Avocado Casserole 57

Chicken Enchilada Soup 58

Portobello Mushrooms Stuffed With Lasagna 60

Pepper And Sausage Soup 62

Thai Zucchini Chicken Soup 64

Veggie Stir Fry 65

Cauliflower And Bell Pepper Soup 67

Cauliflower And Shrimp Curry 69

Crockpot Spicy Lime Garlic Chicken 71

Pork Stew 73

Turkey Lettuce Wraps 75

Vegan Coconut Curry 77

Cheeseburger Salad 79

DINNER 81

Spicy Chicken Chowder 82

Balsamic Chicken 83

Keto Goulash 84

Simple Beef Stew 86

Bacon Topped Meatloaf 87

Cheddar Cheese Broccoli Soup 89

Spicy Chili Soup 91

Lasagna With Zoodles 93

Kale Sausage Soup 94

Spicy Pumpkin Soup 96

Crockpot Butter Chicken 98

Crockpot Beef Curry 100

Vegetable Soup 101

Crockpot Beef Stew 103

Parmesan Coated Pork Chops 105

SNACKS 107

    Coconut And Almond Bark 108

    Pecan Butter Ice Cream 109

    Creamy Cranberry Muffins 111

    Chia Almond Butter Squares 113

    Beef Jerky 115

    Cheese Chips 116

    Low Carb Chocolate Green Smoothie 117

    Creamy Coconut Yogurt 118

    Coconut And Chocolate Fat Bombs 119

    Kale Chips 121

    Green Beans Fries 122

    Avocado Brownies 123

    Sunshine Smoothie 125

    Pesto Crackers 126

    No-Sugar Cheese Parfait With Berries 128

    Pepperoni Chips 129

    Keto Queso Fresco 130

    Spinach Cucumber Smoothie 131

Read Other Books By Nancy Crews:

67 Fruit Infused Water Recipes: Vitamin Water Recipes To Lose Weight, Detox, Boost Immunity And Have A Healthier Body

Clean Eating 4-Week Meal Plan: Clean Eating Beginners Guide With A 28-Day Clean Eating Meal Plan

Family Spiralizer Cookbook: 60 Best Vegetable Spiralizer Recipes, From Breakfast Noodles To Pasta Main Dishes, Fries, Soups, Veggie Sides And Sweet Desserts

Clean Eating Slow Cooker Cookbook: 100 Low-Fuss, Healthy Dinner Recipes With Whole Food Ingredients

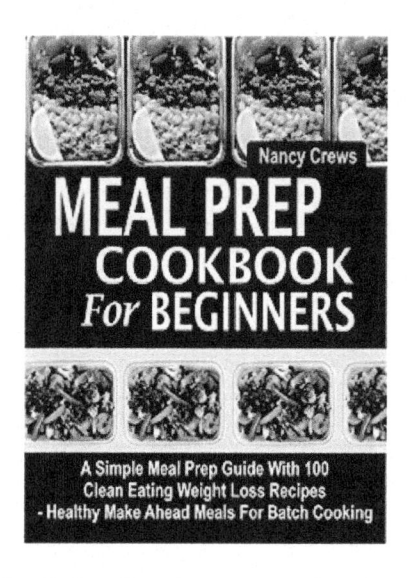

Meal Prep Cookbook For Beginners: A Simple Meal Prep Guide With 100 Clean Eating Weight Loss Recipes - Healthy Make Ahead Meals For Batch Cooking

INTRODUCTION

Staying on the ketogenic diet will be much easier when you incorporate meal prep into your weight loss strategy. With just a few hours of meal prepping on the weekend, you can have budget friendly ketogenic meals that you can eat for the rest of the week. It takes a while to get used to but once you try it a few times, you will be hooked!

The Meal Prep Ketogenic Cookbook contains delicious low carb recipes that are easy to make. The meals you will cook will taste much better than anything you can get from a store or restaurant. They will save you money and you will get the satisfaction of eating your own home cooked meals. What's more, you will be sure of the nutrition your body is getting.

The ketogenic recipes in this book have about 10 grams or less carbs per serving and will help you to prepare delicious food ahead of time. Meal prepping is recommended for people who want to be in control of their body's weight loss process through the ketogenic diet. The recipes in the Meal Prep Ketogenic Cookbook are arranged in categories so you can simply look through the table of content, go to the category you want and choose the recipe you want to cook.

The ketogenic recipes in this book are sugar free and the nutritional information of every recipe is clearly written so you can know how many grams of carbs are in each serving. Staying in nutritional ketosis is easy when you eat the amount of carbohydrates that is right for your body. Use the nutritional information to guide you as you experiment with these recipes to find out the ones that are best for you. You can also adjust the amounts of the ingredients to suit your taste or to get even lower carbohydrate count.

A sample two week meal plan is provided in this section to show you how to plan meals with the recipes in this book. Start with this meal plan and later come up with your own with your the recipes that have become your favorite.

Meal Prep Benefits

Planning your meals gives you a lot of advantages. Below are some of the pecks of meal planning:

1. ***Saves You Time.*** Although you have to invest some time up front, you can easily prepare a week's worth of meals within one or two hours. This is the secret of the mass production industry. When you cook a batch of meals at once, you save several extra hours within the week.

2. ***Makes It Easier To Eat Moderately.*** Overeating is a battle many dieters keep fighting. Meal prep creates pre-portioned meals and you don't have to keep thinking about the amount of food to eat. It also helps you overcome the emotional urge of going for seconds.

3. ***Reduces The Risk Of Eating Junk Food.*** When you cook your own meals, you know every ingredient that goes in. You can have homemade snacks that you can easily reach for while in the office or in traffic.

4. ***Saves You Money.*** Cooking your own meals at home is almost always cheaper than eating out. Furthermore because you are cooking in batches, you buy groceries in bulk at cheaper prices.

5. ***Narrows Down Decision Making.*** Pre-planning your meals means you just have to think about want to cook for lunch or dinner once or twice a week. You don't have to keep doing this every day. Additionally, the willpower to get into the kitchen and cook is not always there. Planning

ahead eliminates most of the decisions that can derail your health and fitness goals.

Meal Prep Beginners' Guide

Start Small

Don't jump into meal prep by preparing everything you will eat in one week. Start by preparing a few meals ahead of time. Many people are already used to taking their lunches to work so it is easier to start with this. If you are prepping for a family, dinner may be the best to start with. Dinner is also advisable for those who work late. If you don't do much cooking, you can start by prepping just one or two days at a time. If you rush out to work early in the mornings, preparing breakfast will be a great help.

The chopping, cooking and cleaning required for five days' worth of meals can be overwhelming and you can easily give up. Preparing a few meals at a time is also a good way to test each recipe to know the one you like and the portions you can eat. A little bit of trial and error is allowed, so use the first few weeks to find a routine that works for you.

Start with simple meals.

Start with recipes that are easy for you. Most people find it easy to cook chicken dishes and there are several chicken recipes in this book. Chicken can be cooked in an almost endless number of ways. Chicken is also easy to store in the freezer.

Get Necessary Equipment

- Meal Prep Containers: Tupperware, Bento-Style Meal Prep Containers, Mason Jars And Bags

- Aluminum Foil

- Measuring Cups And Spoons

- Mixing Bowls

- Spatula

- Knife

- Baking Sheets

- Cutting Board

- Small Saucepan, Sauté Pan

- Large Pot

- Blender Or Food Processor

- Kitchen Scale

Buy Good Storage Containers

Proper containers are essential to meal prep. Not storing your meals the right way can thwart your meal prepping efforts. The whole point of preparing meals ahead can be defeated if you just throw everything into random bowls.

The ideal container should be airtight with sections divided for different food items. This will give you crispier, fresher and better tasting meals. Containers should also be stackable so you can maximize refrigerator and freezer space. Clear containers or at least those with clear covers are also advantageous. They enable you to quickly see the food that is inside. Additionally, buy containers that are BPA free, microwavable, freezer safe, dishwasher safe, stackable and reusable.

Stock Up On Food

Saturday or Sunday are the best days to do your weekly grocery shopping as well as cooking. This will give you enough time to prepare the meals you need for the work week. Make a list of what you need so you won't forget stuff and waste time going back and forth.

Go through this book and choose the recipes you want to cook for the week. Next, check your fridge and pantry for the items you already have and make a list of the ones you need to buy before heading to the store.

Choose A Day For Cooking

As said earlier, Sunday is a favorite cooking day for many meal preppers. Most people are off work and family members are often around to help. You may also split the weekly prepping into two days. Do some on Sunday and the rest on Wednesday. You can use a calendar to make a visual map of the meals you want to prep each week.

Prep Staples In Bulk

Once you have gained some meal prepping momentum, start preparing staples like chicken in bulk. You will need them over and over. You can easily cook a whole chicken, use some immediately and refrigerate or freeze the remainder.

Tips For Making Meal Prep Easy

Write Down A Plan For Each Week

Working with a plan will make meal prep work for you. Start by determining the meals you want to cook, choose the recipes then make a list of needed ingredients. Add storage containers and other necessities to your list. Make sure everything is ready before you start cooking. It is also important to have enough space in your refrigerator or freezer.

In addition check your calendar to determine your movement within the upcoming week. For instance, if you are having a dinner meeting with a client or an out of town engagement, you may have to cook dinner for just 3 days.

Multitask

Save time by combining meal prepping tasks. For instance, a few different things can be cooked at the same time. You can put more than one baking sheet with different meals in the oven at the same time. You can also use aluminum foil to divide items on the same oven tray. Many recipes can be cooked this way. Multitasking will help you to work variety into meal prepping. Nobody wants to eat the same lunch or dinner for an entire week.

Use No-Cook Recipes

No cook recipes greatly reduce meal prepping time and there are several of them in this book. Salads and smoothies will help you to save time when prepping.

Use Leftovers

A piece of chicken left over from dinner can easily be matched with a salad for lunch the next day. Just store leftovers properly and reheat the next day.

Use A Crockpot Or Pressure Cooker

Slow cookers are popular with meal preppers and many have also started using pressure cookers. They are great time savers because of the set and forget cooking style.

2 WEEK MEAL PLAN

Week 1, Day 1

Breakfast:

- Omelet Roll

Midday snack:

- Coconut And Almond Bark

Lunch:

- Spicy Chili

- 1 lettuce salad

Dinner:

- Spicy Chicken Chowder

- 2 cups of raw baby spinach with ranch dressing

Evening snack:

- A few raw almonds

Week 1, Day 2

Breakfast:

- Egg, Bacon And Cheese Cups

Midday snack:

- Pecan Butter Ice Cream

Lunch:

- Chicken Salad

Dinner:

- Balsamic Chicken

- 2 cups of chopped romaine lettuce with sour cream and shredded cheddar cheese

Evening snack:

- 1/2 avocado seasoned with salt and pepper

Week 1, Day 3

Breakfast:

- Vanilla Smoothie

Midday snack:

- Creamy Cranberry Muffins

Lunch:

- Chili Con Carne

Dinner:

- Keto Goulash

Evening snack:

- 1 or 2 string cheese

Week 1, Day 4

Breakfast:

- Zucchini And Walnut Bread

- Coffee with 2 tablespoons of heavy cream

Midday snack:

- Chia Almond Butter Squares

Lunch:

- Chicken And Cauliflower Casserole

Dinner:

- Beef Stew

- 2 cups of chopped romaine lettuce with sugar free Italian dressing

Evening snack:

- A few sticks of celery with almond butter

Week 1, Day 5

Breakfast:

- Ricotta Blueberry Pancakes

- Coffee with 2 tablespoons of heavy cream

Midday snack:

- Beef Jerky

Lunch:

- Chicken Avocado Casserole

Dinner:

- Bacon Topped Meatloaf

- 2 cups of chopped romaine lettuce with sugar free Italian dressing

Evening Snack:

- A few raw almonds

Week 1, Day 6

Breakfast:

- Breakfast Sausage Casserole

Midday snack:

- Cheese Chips

Lunch:

- Chicken Enchilada Soup

- Lettuce salad

Dinner:

- Cheddar Cheese Broccoli Soup

- 2 slices cooked bacon

Evening snack:

- 1/2 avocado seasoned with salt and pepper

Week 1, Day 7

Breakfast:

- White Pizza Frittata

- Coffee with 2 tablespoons of heavy cream

Midday snack:

- Creamy Coconut Yogurt

Lunch:

- Portobello Mushrooms Stuffed With Lasagna

Dinner:

- Lasagna With Zoodles

Evening snack:

- 1 or 2 string cheese

Week 2, Day 1

Breakfast:

- Quiche With Almond Crust

- 1 cup of Pepper And Sausage Soup

Midday snack:

- Creamy Coconut Yogurt

Lunch:

- Pepper And Sausage Soup

Dinner:

- Kale Sausage Soup

Evening snack:

- A few sticks of celery with almond butter

Week 2, Day 2

Breakfast:

- Creamy Cheese Pancakes

- Coffee with 2 tablespoons of heavy cream

Midday snack:

- Coconut And Chocolate Fat Bombs

Lunch:

- Thai Zucchini Chicken Soup

- Lettuce salad

Dinner:

- Spicy Pumpkin Soup

- Side salad

Evening snack:

- A few raw almonds

Week 2, Day 3

Breakfast:

- Feta, Spinach And Sausage Frittata

- Coffee with 2 tablespoons of heavy cream

Midday snack:

- Kale Chips

Lunch:

- Veggie Stir Fry

Dinner:

- Crockpot Butter Chicken

- 2 cups of chopped romaine lettuce with sour cream and shredded cheddar cheese

Evening snack:

- 1/2 avocado seasoned with salt and pepper

Week 2, Day 4

Breakfast:

- Chocolate Smoothie

Midday snack:

- Green Beans Fries

Lunch:

- Cauliflower And Bell Pepper Soup

Dinner:

- Crockpot Beef Curry

- 2 cups of chopped romaine lettuce with sugar free Italian dressing

Evening snack:

- 1 or 2 string cheese

Week 2, Day 5

Breakfast:

- Egg, Bacon And Cheese Cups

Midday snack:

- Sunshine Smoothie

Lunch:

- Cauliflower And Shrimp Curry

Dinner:

- Vegetable Soup

Evening snack:

- A few sticks of celery with almond butter

Week 2, Day 6

Breakfast:

- Overnight Flaxseed Meal

Midday snack:

- Avocado Brownies

Lunch:

- Crockpot Spicy Lime Garlic Chicken

- Side salad

Dinner:

- Crockpot Beef Stew

- 2 cups of chopped romaine lettuce with sour cream and shredded cheddar cheese

Evening snack:

- A few raw almonds

Week 2, Day 7

Breakfast:

- Breakfast Egg Muffins

Midday snack:

- Pesto Crackers

Lunch:

- Pork Stew

Dinner:

- Parmesan Coated Pork Chops

- Veggie side

Evening snack:

- 1/2 avocado seasoned with salt and pepper

BREAKFAST

Egg, Bacon And Cheese Cups
Take them with you wherever you go.

Servings: 12

Preparation time: 10 minutes

Cooking time: 15 minutes

Ingredients:

12 large eggs

12 strips of bacon

1/2 cup of frozen spinach, thawed and drained

1/3 cup of sharp cheddar cheese

Salt

Pepper

Directions:

1. Preheat oven to 400F.

2. Fry the bacon in a pan. When it is done, keep aside on a cooling rack so as to drain the excess oil.

3. Generously grease a 12-cup muffin pan with either olive or coconut oil. Use a slice of bacon to line each of the cups and press down so that the slice sticks up on both sides.

4. Beat the eggs in a large bowl lightly.

5. Using paper towel, drain out any excess water from the spinach. Add the spinach to the beaten eggs and stir.

6. Spoon 1/4 cup of the egg mix into each of the muffin cups. Fill the cup about 3/4 of the way.

7. Evenly sprinkle the cheese on top. Season with salt and pepper.

8. Bake for 15 minutes on the middle rack.

Storage: Keep in an airtight container in the fridge for 1 week.

Usage: Heat up in the microwave

Nutrition Per Serving:

Calories: 101, Fat: 7g, Protein: 8g, Carb: 1g

Omelet Roll
With these omelet, you won't miss burritos.

Servings: 3

Preparation time: 10 minutes

Cooking time: 20 minutes

Ingredients:

3 ounces lean ground turkey

1 large egg

4 egg whites

1/3 cup diced bell pepper

1 handful of spinach

1 ounce of goat cheese

Salt and pepper to taste

Directions:

1. Season the ground turkey with salt and pepper. Cook in a skillet until brown, drain.

2. In another pan, cook the whole egg and the egg whites.

3. Add the ground turkey, bell pepper, spinach and goat cheese.

4. Roll up and serve.

Storage: Seal in plastic wrap and keep in the fridge for 2-3 days.

Usage: Heat up in the microwave on very low heat.

Nutrition Per Serving:

Calories: 350, Fat: 11g, Protein: 50g, Carbs: 1g

Vanilla Smoothie

Quick to make and extremely filling.

Servings: 1

Preparation time: 2 minutes

Cooking time: 0 minutes

Ingredients:

1/2 cup of full-fat mascarpone cheese

1/4 cup of water

4 ice cubes

2 large egg yolks

1 tablespoon of coconut oil

1 tablespoon of powdered erythritol

1/2 teaspoon of pure vanilla extract

Whipped cream, optional

Directions:

1. Blend all the ingredients except the whipped cream together in a blender.

2. Process until it is smooth.

3. Add the whipped cream as topping.

Storage: Store in a glass container with an airtight lid. Will keep for 1-2 days.

Usage: Drink whenever you want.

Nutrition Per Serving:

Calories: 650, Fat: 64g, Protein: 12g, Carbs: 4g.

Zucchini And Walnut Bread

Turn breakfast into a nice treat.

Servings: 16

Preparation time: 20 minutes

Cooking time: 1 hour 10 minutes

Ingredients:

2 1/2 cups of almond flour

1 1/2 cups of erythritol

1 cup of zucchini, grated

1/2 cup of olive oil

1/2 cup of walnuts, chopped

3 large eggs

1 1/2 teaspoons baking powder

1 teaspoon of vanilla extract

1 teaspoon of ground cinnamon

½ teaspoon nutmeg

1/2 teaspoon of salt

¼ teaspoon ground ginger

Directions:

1. Preheat the oven to 350F.

2. In a bowl, whisk the eggs, vanilla extract and oil together. Keep aside.

3. Combine the baking powder, almond flour, cinnamon, erythritol, nutmeg, ginger and salt in another bowl. Keep aside.

4. Wring excess water from the zucchini with a paper towel or cheese cloth. Add the zucchini to the egg mixture and whisk together.

5. Using a hand mixer, add the flour mixture to the egg mixture slowly until it is well blended.

6. Grease a 9x5 loaf pan lightly and scoop the dough into it.

7. Add the walnuts as toppings. Use a spatula to press the walnuts into the dough.

8. Bake for 60-70 minutes or until the walnuts turn brown.

Storage: Wrap bread in foil, plastic wrap or freezer bag and freeze. Will keep for 1-2 months.

Usage: Heat in microwave

Nutrition Per Serving:

Calories: 201.1, Fat: 18.9g, Protein: 5.6g, Carb: 2.5g

Ricotta Blueberry Pancakes
A delicious keto-compliant recipe.

Servings: 5

Preparation time: 10 minutes

Cooking time: 15 minutes

Ingredients:

1 cup of almond flour

½ cup of golden flaxseed meal

¼ cup of unsweetened vanilla almond milk

¼ cup of blueberries

¾ cup of ricotta

3 large eggs

1 teaspoon of baking powder

½ teaspoon of vanilla extract

¼-½ teaspoon of stevia powder

¼ teaspoon of salt

Directions:

1. Over medium heat, preheat a skillet.

2. Blend the almond milk, eggs, vanilla extract and ricotta together in a blender.

3. In another bowl, combine the baking powder, flaxseed meal, almond flour, stevia and salt together.

4. Add this flour mixture to the egg mixture in the blender slowly. Process until it forms a smooth dough.

5. Concerning the blueberries, add 2-3 blueberries to each pancake.

6. Melt butter in the skillet. Add the dough to the pan and turn when its outside browns lightly.

Storage: Wrap each pancake in plastic wrap, and keep in the freezer for about 3 weeks.

Usage: Heat in microwave.

Nutrition Per Serving:

Calories: 296.6, Fats: 22.6g, Protein: 13.4g, Carbs: 5.9g.

Breakfast Sausage Casserole

Start of your morning on the right note with this yummy dish.

Servings: 6

Preparation time: 15 minutes

Cooking time: 40 minutes

Ingredients:

1 pound of pork sausage

2 cups of green cabbage, shredded

1 medium onion, diced

2 cups of zucchini, chopped

1 1/2 cups of shredded cheddar cheese, divided

1/2 cup of mayonnaise

3 large eggs

2 teaspoons of prepared yellow mustard

1 teaspoon of dried ground sage

Cayenne pepper

Directions:

1. Preheat oven to 375F. Grease a casserole dish and keep aside.

2. In a large pan, brown the sausage over medium heat until it is almost cooked.

3. Add the zucchini, cabbage and onion to the pan. Cook until the sausage is well cooked and the veggies are soft.

4. Remove from heat. Spoon the mixture into the casserole dish and keep aside.

5. Whisk the eggs, mustards, pepper, mayonnaise and sage in a bowl until the mixture is smooth.

6. Add a cup of the cheese to the mixture and stir to combine. Pour this mixture over the sausage and veggies in the casserole dish.

7. Add the remaining cheese as topping.

8. Bake for 30 minutes or until the cheese melts and turns light brown on top and it is bubbly around its edges.

9. Serve immediately.

Storage: Divide into portion and freeze in an airtight container for 1-2 weeks.

Usage: Heat in a microwave

Nutrition Per Serving:

Calories: 487, Fat: 41.94g, Protein: 19.11g, Carb: 4.78g.

Lemon Poppyseed Muffins

Rich, moist and nutritious.

Servings: 12

Preparation time: 15 minutes

Cooking time: 20 minutes

Ingredients:

1/4 cup of heavy cream

1/4 cup of flaxseed meal

1/4 cup of melted salted butter

1/3 cup of erythritol

3/4 cup of almond flour

3 large eggs

3 tablespoons of lemon juice

2 tablespoons of poppy seeds

1 teaspoon of vanilla extract

1 teaspoon of baking powder

Zest of 2 lemons

25 drops of liquid stevia

Directions:

1. Preheat oven to 350F.

2. Combine flaxseed meal, poppy seeds, almond flour and erythritol in a bowl.

3. Stir in the eggs, butter and cream until it forms a smooth paste.

4. Add in the vanilla extract, lemon zest, baking powder, lemon juice and stevia to the bowl. Stir to combine everything thoroughly.

5. Evenly divide the dough among 12 cupcake molds.

6. Bake for 18-20 minutes or until it browns slightly.

7. Remove from oven, allow to cool for about 10 minutes and serve.

Storage: Keep in an airtight container and refrigerate for a week or freeze for 1-2 months.

Usage: Heat in microwave.

Nutrition Per Serving:

Calories: 129, Fats: 11.3g, Protein 3.7g, Carbs: 1.5g

White Pizza Frittata

An excuse to have pizza for breakfast.

Servings: 8

Preparation time: 15 minutes

Cooking time: 30 minutes

Ingredients:

1 (9-ounce) bag of frozen spinach

5 ounces of mozzarella cheese

1 ounce of pepperoni

12 large eggs

1/2 cup of parmesan cheese

1/2 cup of fresh ricotta cheese

4 tablespoons of olive oil

1 teaspoon of garlic, minced

1/4 teaspoon of nutmeg

Salt

Pepper

Directions:

1. Thaw the spinach in a microwave for about 3 minutes. Wring the spinach with your hands to drain the excess water. Keep aside.

2. Preheat oven to 375F.

3. In a bowl, combine the olive oil, eggs and spices together. Add in the parmesan, ricotta and spinach. Break the spinach into small pieces when adding it.

4. Pour the mixture into a cast iron pan and top with a sprinkling of the mozzarella. Top with the pepperoni.

5. Bake for 30 minutes. Slice and serve.

Storage: Put in a freezer bag and freeze for up to 1 month.

Usage: Heat in microwave.

Nutrition Per Serving:

Calories: 298, Fats: 23.8g, Protein: 19.4g, Carb: 2.1g.

Quiche With Almond Crust
Crusty on the outside, moist on the inside.

Servings: 8

Preparation time: 10 minutes

Cooking time: 45 minutes

Ingredients:

1 1/2 cups of almond flour

1 1/2 cups of cheddar cheese

1/4 cup of olive oil plus 1 teaspoon, if desired

1/4 teaspoon of salt

6 large eggs

6 slices of bacon, cut into chunks

1 teaspoon of dried oregano

1 teaspoon of Mrs. Dash table blend

1 teaspoon of garlic

1 green bell pepper

1/2 teaspoon of pepper

1/4 teaspoon of salt

Directions:

1. Preheat oven to 350F.

2. Cook the bacon chunks in a pan.

3. In a bowl, mix the almond flour, olive oil, oregano and 1/4 teaspoon of salt together. Knead dough and shape into a ball. Press the batter into an 11x7 casserole dish.

4. Bake for 20 minutes.

5. Transfer the cooked bacon to paper towels to cool. Sauté the garlic and green peppers in the bacon pan.

6. Add the cheese, table blend, eggs, bacon, garlic, pepper, salt, green pepper and bacon fat. Combine well and pour this mixture into the crust.

7. Bake for 15-18 minutes and remove to cool.

Storage: Cover with plastic wrap or aluminum foil and refrigerate for 3-4 days or freeze for 2-3 months.

Usage: Heat in oven or microwave.

Nutrition Per Serving:

Calories: 331, Fats: 4.1g, Protein: 11.3g, Carbs: 4.1g.

Creamy Cheese Pancakes

The perfect breakfast pancakes.

Servings: 4

Preparation time: 5 minutes

Cooking time: 12 minutes

Ingredients:

2 ounces of cream cheese

1 teaspoon of stevia

2 eggs

1/2 teaspoon of cinnamon

Directions:

1. Blend all the ingredients in a blender until smooth. Keep aside for 2 minutes so that the bubbles can settle.

2. Grease a pan with pam spray or butter, heat then pour about 1/4 of the batter in the hot pan.

3. Cook for 2 minutes until it turns golden, flip and cook the other side for 1 minute. Do this for the rest of the batter.

4. Serve with berries and your preferred syrup.

Storage: Wrap each pancake in a plastic wrap and store in freezer for about 1 month.

Usage: Heat in microwave.

Nutrition Per Serving:

Calories: 344, Fat: 29g, Protein: 17g, Carb: 3g

Feta, Spinach And Sausage Frittata
This keeps extremely well in the fridge.

Servings: 18

Preparation time: 15 minutes

Cooking time: 30 minutes

Ingredients:

1 (10-ounce) package of frozen spinach, thawed, chopped and drained

12 ounces of sausage

12 eggs

1/2 cup of feta cheese, crumbled

1/2 cup of plain unsweetened almond milk

1/2 cup of heavy cream

1/4 teaspoon of ground nutmeg

1/2 teaspoon of salt

1/4 teaspoon of black pepper

Directions:

1. Break the sausage into little pieces and keep in a medium-size bowl.

2. Wring out excess liquid from the spinach and break it into small pieces while adding to the sausage. Sprinkle the feta cheese on top and lightly toss until it well mixed.

3. Grease an 18-cup muffin pan and spoon the sausage mixture lightly into the bottom of the cups.

4. Whisk the eggs, almond milk, cream, nutmeg, pepper and salt in a large bowl until it is well-mixed. Pour into the cups gently until it is about 3/4 full.

5. Bake for 30 minutes at 375F or until it is fully set. Serve either warm or at room temperature.

Storage: Place in an airtight container or freezer bag and freeze for up to a month.

Usage: Heat in microwave.

Nutrition Per Serving:

Calories: 137, Fat: 10g, Protein: 8g, Carb: 1g

Chocolate Smoothie

If you love a cold breakfast, this is the ideal recipe.

Servings: 2

Preparation time: 5 minutes

Cooking time: 0 minutes

Ingredients:

3 cups of crushed ice

1/2 cup of almond milk

1/2 cup of raspberries

1/4 cup of chopped walnuts

1/3 cup of vanilla whey protein powder

2 tablespoons of pomegranate arils

1 tablespoon of melted coconut oil

1 tablespoon of cocoa powder

1/8 teaspoon of xanthan gum

Sweetener

Directions:

1. Put the almond milk in a blender cup.

2. Add in the cocoa powder, sweetener, protein powder, and thickener if desired. Top with the ice and process.

3. Pour in the coconut oil while the blender is still running. Keep blending until it almost doubles in volume. Adjust taste to your preference.

4. Pour the smoothie into a bowl. Add fruits and nuts as toppings. Serve!

Storage: Keep refrigerated in a covered glass jar for 2 days.

Usage: Remove from fridge and serve.

Nutrition Per Serving:

Calories: 280, Fat: 16g, Protein: 25g, Carb: 7g

No-Flour Waffles

Make these super delicious waffles with just 4 ingredients.

Servings: 4

Preparation time: 5 minutes

Cooking time: 10 minutes

Ingredients:

1/2 cup of almond butter

4 large eggs

1 tablespoon of erythritol

1/2 teaspoon of gluten-free baking powder

Directions:

1. Using either a food processor, blender or hand mixer, process all the ingredients together until you have a smooth paste.

2. Lightly grease a waffle maker with butter or oil and preheat.

3. Wait for the bubbles in the batter to settle then pour the batter into the waffle maker and cook according to manufacturer's instructions.

Storage: Wrap waffles individually in plastic bags and freeze for up to 3 months.

Usage: Heat in microwave.

Nutrition Per Serving:

Calories: 264, Fat: 22g, Protein: 14g, Carb: 6g

Overnight Flaxseed Meal

Healthy and delicious.

Servings: 2

Preparation time: 5 minutes

Cooking time: 0 minutes

Ingredients:

1/2 cup of flaxseed meal

1/2 cup of yogurt

1/3 cup of unsweetened almond milk

3/4 cup of raspberries

3 tablespoons of sweetener

3 tablespoons of vanilla protein powder

Directions:

1. Mix all the ingredients in a mason jar until it well combined.

2. Keep in fridge for 4-5 hours or overnight.

Storage: Refrigerate for 1-2 days.

Usage: Remove from fridge and serve.

Nutrition Per Serving:

Calories: 249, Protein: 23.7g, Carb: 4.9g

Cauliflower Herbed Egg Muffins

A delicious recipe filled with healthy ingredients.

Servings: 10

Preparation time: 20 minutes

Cooking time: 20 minutes

Ingredients:

2 cups of cauliflower, riced

1 cup of cheese, shredded, divided

1/2 cup of gluten-free flour

8 eggs

1/2 teaspoon of baking powder

1/2 teaspoon of oregano

1/2 teaspoon of pepper

1/2 teaspoon of basil

1/2 teaspoon of salt

1/4 teaspoon of dried dill

Directions:

1. Preheat oven to 350F.

2. Using either silicone or parchment liners, line a muffin pan and keep aside.

3. Combine the basil, cauliflower, oregano, eggs, dills, 1/2 cup of cheese, salt and pepper in a large bowl until well-mixed.

4. Add the baking powder and flour. Stir until fully mixed.

5. Scoop the mixture into the muffin pan until it is almost full. Sprinkle the top with the remaining cheese.

6. Bake for 20-25 minutes until the muffins are thoroughly baked and set.

Storage: Refrigerate in an airtight container for up to 5 days or freeze for up to 3 months.

Usage: Heat in microwave.

Nutrition Per Serving:

Calories: 139, Fat: 9g, Fat: 9g, Protein: 9g, Carb: 6g

Breakfast Egg Muffins
A healthy alternative to classic muffins.

Servings: 10

Preparation time: 15 minutes

Cooking time: 25 minutes

Ingredients:

2 cups of mixed vegetables, cubed

1 cup of cheese, shredded, divided

1/2 cup of gluten-free flour

8 eggs

1/2 teaspoon of baking powder

1/2 teaspoon of salt

1/2 teaspoon of pepper

Directions:

1. Preheat oven to 350F.

2. Using a parchment or silicone liner, line a muffin pan and keep aside.

3. Combine the vegetables, eggs, 1/2 cup of cheese, salt and pepper in a large bowl.

4. Add the baking powder and flour. Stir to thoroughly mix.

5. Scoop the mixture into the muffin pan until it is almost full. Sprinkle the top with the remaining cheese.

6. Bake for 20-25 minutes until the muffins are thoroughly baked and set.

Storage: Refrigerate in an airtight container for 5 days or freeze for up to 3 months.

Usage: Heat in microwave.

Nutrition Per Serving:

Calories: 152, Fat: 9g, Protein: 9g, Carb: 8g

Brownie Muffins
Dark, yummy and filling.

Servings: 6

Preparation time: 10 minutes

Cooking time: 15 minutes

Ingredients:

1 cup of flaxseed meal

1/2 cup of pumpkin puree

1/4 cup of cocoa powder

1/4 cup of no-sugar caramel syrup

1/4 cup of slivered almonds

1 large egg

2 tablespoons of coconut oil

1 tablespoon of cinnamon

1/2 tablespoon of baking powder

1 teaspoon of apple cider vinegar

1 teaspoon of vanilla extract

1/2 teaspoon of salt

Directions:

1. Preheat oven to 350F.

2. In a deep bowl, mix together all the ingredients except the almonds.

3. Use 6 paper liners to line a muffin pan and scoop about 1/4 cup of the batter into each liner.

4. Sprinkle the almonds over each muffin top and press gently so that the almonds stick.

5. Bake for about 15 minutes until the muffins rise and set.

Storage: Refrigerate in an airtight container for 1 week or freeze for 3 months.

Usage: Heat in a microwave.

Nutrition Per Serving:

Calories: 183g, Fats: 13.4g, Protein: 7g, Carbs: 3.3g

Pumpkin Pancakes

A comforting breakfast.

Servings: 8

Preparation time: 10 minutes

Cooking time: 5 minutes

Ingredients:

1 cup of almond meal

1/4 cup of sour cream

1/4 cup of pumpkin puree

2 large eggs

2 tablespoons of butter

1 teaspoon of baking powder

1 teaspoon of pumpkin pie spice

1/4 teaspoon of salt

Directions:

1. In a bowl, combine the pumpkin, eggs, butter and sour cream.

2. In another bowl, combine the almond meal, baking powder, pumpkin spice and salt.

3. Add the wet ingredients to the dry ingredients slowly. Mix until smooth.

4. Place a cast iron pan over medium heat and grease it with butter.

5. Scoop 1/3 cup of the batter for each pancake.

6. Flip the pancakes when they begin to bubble at the top. Ensure that the edges are a bit browned.

7. Flip the pancakes and cook for an extra 1 minute. Ensure that both sides are browned.

Storage: Keep in an airtight container or wrap individually in a plastic wrap. Keeps in the refrigerator for 2-3 days or freeze for 2 months.

Usage: Heat in microwave.

Nutrition Per Serving:

Calories: 151, Fats: 12.8g, Protein: 5.4g, Carbs: 1.9g

Chicken Omelet
Adds variety to your normal breakfast.

Servings: 1

Preparation time: 5 minutes

Cooking time: 10 minutes

Ingredients:

1 ounce of deli cut chicken

2 eggs

2 slices of cooked bacon, chopped

1 tablespoon of mustard

1 tablespoon of mayo

1 camapari tomato

1/4 avocado, sliced

Directions:

1. In a small bowl, beat the eggs and add to a hot pan. Season with salt and pepper.

2. When the eggs are cooked halfway, add the bacon, tomato, chicken, avocado, a squirt of mustard and 1 tablespoon of mayo to one half of the eggs.

3. Fold the eggs over itself and cover the pan. Cook for an extra 5 minutes.

Storage: Keep in an airtight container and refrigerate for up to 2 days.

Usage: Heat in microwave

Nutrition Per Serving:

Calories: 415, Fat: 32g, Protein: 25g, Carb: 4g

Homemade Patties
A tasty and healthy breakfast patty.

Servings: 8

Preparation time:

Cooking time:

Ingredients:

1 pound of ground pork

1 tablespoon of olive oil

1 teaspoon of garlic powder

1 teaspoon of fennel seeds

1 teaspoon of salt

1 teaspoon of dried sage

1/4 teaspoon of red pepper flakes

Directions:

1. Combine all the ingredients except the oil in a small bowl.

2. Form meat balls with a large cookie scoop, about 3 tablespoon each. To make the patties, flatten the balls with your hands until the balls are less than 1/2-inch thick. You should have 8 patties.

3. Over medium high heat, heat a cast iron skillet and add the oil.

4. Add the patties and cook for about 5 minutes on each side until they turn golden brown.

5. Drain the patties on a paper towel and serve.

Storage: Freeze patties in a freezer bag or airtight container for up to 6 months.

Usage: Thaw and heat in oven or microwave.

Nutrition Per Serving:

Calories: 186, Protein: 14.7g, Fat: 13.5g, Carb: 0.6g

LUNCH

Spicy Chili

Add some spice to lunch break with this delicious recipe.

Servings: 4

Preparation time: 15 minutes

Cooking time: 4 hours

Ingredients:

1 1/2 pounds of ground beef

1 tablespoon of butter

1/2 can of green chili

3 celery stems, chopped

1/2 medium red onion, chopped

2 cups of broccoli

1 cup of beef broth

1 1/2 cans of tomato with jalapeno

1 ½ teaspoon garlic

2 teaspoons of chili powder

2 teaspoons of cumin

1 teaspoon of Italian seasoning

1 teaspoon of paprika

1 teaspoon of onion powder

Directions:

1. Place a pan over high heat, heat the butter and brown the beef. Season with pepper and salt.

2. In another pan, boil the broccoli.

3. Add half of the onion once the beef begins to sizzle. Stir and keep cooking until the onions caramelize.

4. Put the celery, green chili, 1 can of tomato and celery in a crockpot along with all the spices. Stir and keep aside.

5. Remove the beef from heat. Drain the broccoli and add it to the crockpot.

6. Add the beef with its fat to the crockpot.

7. Stir to combine. Cook for 20 minutes on high heat.

8. Add the remaining ingredients and cook for an extra 3 hours.

Storage: Put in an airtight container and refrigerate for 3-4 days or freeze for 4-6 months.

Usage: Heat in microwave or stove top.

Nutrition Per Serving:

Calories: 539, Fats: 30.5g, Protein: 50g, Carbs: 9.2g

Chicken Salad

Filling and extremely tasty.

Servings: 3

Preparation time: 20 minutes

Cooking time: 0 minutes

Ingredients:

5 ounces roasted chicken breast

1/3 cup of mayonnaise

1 large hardboiled egg

1 green onion

1 rib of celery

2 tablespoons of Italian parsley

1/2 tablespoon of dill relish

1 teaspoon of Dijon mustard

1/8 teaspoon of granulated garlic

Freshly ground black pepper

Kosher salt

Directions:

1. Add chicken to a food processor and pulse until fine. Transfer to a mixing bowl.

2. Add the green onion, celery and parsley to the food processor and pulse until very fine. Add veggies to the chicken bowl.

3. Grate eggs and add to the bowl as well.

4. Add the remaining ingredients with salt and pepper to taste. Stir with a large spoon to incorporate thoroughly.

Storage: Refrigerate in an airtight container for up to a week.

Usage: Serve on top of a salad or bread or buns.

Nutrition Per Serving:

Calories: 283, Fat: 23g, Protein: 16g, Carb: 1g

Chili Con Carne
This comfort food is amazingly low carb!

Servings: 5

Preparation time: 10 minutes

Cooking time: 2 hours 35 minutes

Ingredients:

1 pound of hot Italian sausage

1 pound of ground beef

1 can of tomato sauce

1 large yellow pepper, chopped

1 large green pepper, chopped

1 medium white onion, chopped

2 tablespoons of cumin

2 tablespoons of chili powder

2 tablespoons of curry powder

1 tablespoon of butter

1 tablespoon of organic coconut oil

1 tablespoon of garlic, minced

1 teaspoon of freshly ground black pepper

1 teaspoon of onion powder

1 teaspoon of salt

Directions:

1. Heat a pan over medium high and add the coconut oil and butter.

2. Saute the onions, peppers and garlic with frequent stirring.

3. Heat a pot over medium and brown the ground beef and sausage. Season with salt and pepper.

4. Mix the sauteed vegetables with the beef mixture. Add the tomato sauce, chili powder and onion powder. Stir and cook for 20 minutes.

5. Add the cumin and curry powder. Cook for an additional 10 minutes while stirring frequently.

6. Leave to simmer for 45 minutes to 2 hours.

Storage: Keep in an airtight container or plastic bag and refrigerate for 3-4 days or freeze for 4-6 months.

Usage: Heat in microwave.

Nutrition Per Serving:

Calories: 415, Fat: 25g, Carb: 6g.

Chicken And Cauliflower Casserole

A truly delightful casserole.

Servings: 10

Preparation time: 20 minutes

Cooking time: 1 hour 30 minutes

Ingredients:

12 chicken thighs, cut up

6 bacon slices

8 ounces of shredded Monterey Jack cheese

8 ounces of shredded cheddar cheese

8 ounces of cream cheese

4 ounces of heavy cream

6 green onions, chopped

1 cauliflower head, chopped into florets

1 green pepper, chopped

1 medium onion, chopped

1 tablespoon of garlic, minced

Salt

Pepper

Directions:

1. Add the chicken to pot. Add some water and season with salt and pepper. Cook until done on the stovetop.

2. Cook the bacon in the oven at 450F for 15-20 minutes.

3. Put the cauliflower in the microwave and cook on vegetable setting.

4. Fry the onions and vegetables in a pan.

5.Transfer cooked chicken to a large bowl. Add all the ingredients including the fried veggies and cauliflower while reserving 2 ounces of Monterey jack and cheddar cheese each.

6. Transfer the mixture to a large casserole that has been greased. Top with the reserved cheese.

6. Cover the dish with foil and cook in the oven at 350F for 25 minutes. Remove the foil and cook for additional 5 minutes.

Storage: Store in an oven-proof container and freeze for up to 4 months.

Usage: Heat in oven.

Nutrition Per Serving:

Calories:516, Fat: 34g, Protein: 44g, Carb: 9g

Chicken Avocado Casserole

Enjoy this yummy dish all through the weekend.

Servings: 6

Preparation time: 15 minutes

Cooking time: 20 minutes

Ingredients:

8 cooked chicken thighs, boneless

8 ounces of cheddar cheese

8 ounces of sour cream

4 small avocados, peeled, halved and sliced into thin strips

1 medium pepper, cut into strips

1 medium onion, cut into strips

1 tablespoon of hot sauce

Salt

Pepper

Directions:

1. Preheat oven to 350F.

2. Line the bottom of a greased baking dish with the avocado slices.

3. Fry the pepper and onion strips in a pan until it caramelizes.

4. Put the chicken in a large bowl and flake it apart. Add the rest of the ingredients and combine.

5. Spoon the chicken mixture over the slices of avocado.

6. Bake for 20 minutes.

Storage: Keep in an airtight container and refrigerate for up to 2 days or freeze for 1 month.

Usage: Heat in oven or microwave.

Nutrition Per Serving:

Calories: 549, Fat: 40g, Protein: 39g, Carb: 13g

Chicken Enchilada Soup
Enjoy this creamy and sumptuous goodness for lunch.

Servings: 4

Preparation time: 15 minutes

Cooking time: 52 minutes

Ingredients:

8 ounces of cream cheese

6 ounces of chicken, shredded

4 cups of chicken broth

1 cup of chopped tomatoes

1/2 cup of chopped cilantro

3 celery stalks, chopped

1 red bell pepper, chopped

3 tablespoons of olive oil

2 teaspoons of cumin

2 teaspoons of crushed garlic

1 teaspoon of chili powder

1 teaspoon of oregano

1/2 teaspoon of cayenne pepper

Juice of 1/2 medium lime

Salt

Pepper

Directions:

1. Heat oil in a pan and sauté the bell peppers, garlic and celery. Add the tomatoes once the celery is soft and cook for 2-3 minutes.

2. Add all the spices and stir to combine.

3. Add the cilantro and chicken broth. Leave to boil, reduce heat to low and simmer for 20 minutes.

4. Add the cream cheese and allow to boil. Turn down the heat to low and leave to simmer for 25 minutes.

5. Add the shredded chicken and the lime juice. Combine.

6. Sprinkle shredded cheese, cilantro or sour cream on top and serve.

Storage: Keep in an airtight container and refrigerate for up to 2 days or freeze for 3-4 months.

Usage: Heat in microwave.

Nutrition Per Serving:

Calories: 404.5, Fat: 33.3g, Protein: 13.3g, Carbs: 8.8g

Portobello Mushrooms Stuffed With Lasagna
Tastes absolutely terrific.

Servings: 4

Preparation time: 15 minutes

Cooking time: 20 minutes

Ingredients:

4 large Portobello mushrooms, stemmed, gills removed

1 1/2 cups of spinach, chopped

1 1/2 cups of light ricotta

1 cup of mozzarella, shredded

1 cup of marinara sauce

1/2 cup of basil, chopped

1 egg

1-2 tablespoons of olive oil

1/4 teaspoon of salt

Directions:

1. Preheat oven to 400F.

2. Line a baking pan with parchment paper or use a baking dish to trap the juice from the mushroom.

3. Wash the mushrooms and leave to dry. Use olive oil to brush the insides and tops.

4. Scoop 1/4 cup of marinara sauce into each of the mushrooms.

5. Combine salt, spinach, ricotta, egg and basil in a medium bowl. Evenly divide this mixture among the mushrooms.

6. Sprinkle 1/4 cup of mozzarella on each mushroom.

7. Bake for 20 minutes or until the mushrooms are done.

Storage: Allow mushroom to cool completely, wrap each of the mushroom in foil and put in an airtight container. Freeze for up to 3 months.

Usage: Heat oven to 350F. Place frozen mushroom in a baking pan, cover with foil and bake for 50 minutes or until the cheese bubbles and it is well-heated.

Nutrition Per Serving:

Calories: 261, Fat: 16g, Protein: 21g, Carb: 11g

Pepper And Sausage Soup
Spicy and super-delicious.

Servings: 4

Preparation time: 10 minutes

Cooking time: 55 minutes

Ingredients:

2 pounds of pork sausage

10 ounces of raw spinach

1 can of tomatoes with jalapenos

4 cups of beef stock

1 medium green bell pepper, sliced into pieces

1 tablespoon of olive oil

1 tablespoon of cumin

1 tablespoon of chili powder

1 teaspoon of Italian seasoning

1 teaspoon of onion powder

1 teaspoon of garlic powder

3/4 teaspoon of kosher salt

Directions:

1. In a large pot, heat oil over medium heat. Add the sausage and cook until it is seared. Stir and keep cooking.

2. Add the pieces of green pepper and stir. Season with pepper and salt.

3. Add the can of tomatoes with jalapenos and stir. Top with the spinach and cover the pot.

4. Wait for the spinach to wilts then add the broth and spices. Stir to combine together then add more salt and pepper.

5. Cover and cook for 30 minutes while turning down the heat to medium-low.

6. When it is done, uncover and leave to simmer for 15 minutes.

Storage: Refrigerate in a covered container for 1 week or freeze for up to 4 months.

Usage: Heat on a stovetop or microwave.

Nutrition Per Serving:

Calories: 526, Fats: 43g, Protein: 27.8g, Carbs: 3.8g

Thai Zucchini Chicken Soup

A hearty and yummy Thai delicacy.

Servings: 8

Preparation time: 10 minutes

Cooking time: 20 minutes

Ingredients:

1 (15-ounce) can of full fat coconut milk

1 pound of chicken thighs or breasts, sliced thinly against the grain

6 cups of chicken bone broth

1/2 cup of cilantro, chopped

2 garlic cloves, minced

2 medium zucchini, spiralized

1 red pepper, sliced thinly

1 jalapeno, chopped

1/2 onion, chopped

2 tablespoons of fish sauce

1 1/2 tablespoons of green curry paste

1 tablespoon of coconut oil

1 lime, cut into 8 wedges

Directions:

1. Heat oil in a large pan over medium heat until it melts and become shimmery. Sauté the onions for about 5 minutes or until translucent.

2. Stir in the curry paste, jalapeno and garlic. Sauté for about 1 minute until it becomes fragrant.

3. Add the coconut milk and broth. Whisk until it is well mixed. Allow to boil and turn down the heat to medium.

4. Add the fish sauce, red pepper and chicken. Allow to simmer for about 5 minutes until the chicken is well-cooked. Add the cilantro and stir.

5. Divide the zucchini among 8 bowls and ladle the hot soup over.

6. Serve with a squeeze of lime.

Storage: Keep in a covered container and refrigerate for a day or freeze for 2-3 weeks.

Usage: Heat in microwave.

Nutrition Per Serving:

Calories: 271, Fat: 12.49g, Protein: 24.42g, Carb: 8.91g

Veggie Stir Fry
A fun way to get kids to eat veggies.

Servings: 4

Preparation time: 7 minutes

Cooking time: 10 minutes

Ingredients:

1 cup of cooked chicken

1-2 cups of green beans

1/4 cup of coconut oil

2 garlic cloves, crushed

6 carrots, julienned

1/2 small onion, chopped

3-4 tablespoons of coconut aminos

Sea salt

Pepper

Directions:

1. Heat the oil in a large pan and sauté the onion for about 5 minutes. Season with a pinch or 2 of salt.

2. Add and sauté the garlic for an additional minute.

3. Add the green beans, coconut aminos, carrots and chicken. Cook over medium heat until the vegetables are well cooked.

4. Season with salt and pepper.

Storage: Keep in an airtight container and refrigerate for 2 days or freeze for 1 month.

Usage: Heat in microwave.

Nutrition Per Serving:

Calories: 310, Fat: 23.7g, Protein: 8.7g, Carbs: 9.22g

Cauliflower And Bell Pepper Soup

Very nice when the weather is cold.

Servings: 5

Preparation time: 20 minutes

Cooking time: 1 hour 20 minutes

Ingredients:

3 cups of chicken broth

1/2 cup of heavy cream

1/2 cauliflower head, cut into florets

3 medium green onions, chopped

2 red bell peppers, halved, seed removed

6 tablespoons of duck fat

4 ounce of crumbled goat cheese

1 teaspoon of smoked paprika

1 teaspoon of dried thyme

1 teaspoon of garlic powder

1/4 teaspoon of red pepper flakes

Directions:

1. Broil the bell peppers for 10-15 minutes or until the skin is blackened and charred. Keep in a container and cover to steam.

2. Meanwhile, season the florets with 2 tablespoon of melted duck fat, pepper and salt. Roast in the oven for 30-35 minutes at 400F.

3. Peel the skins off the pepper carefully.

4. Heat the remaining duck fat in a pot and add the green onion. Add the seasonings to toast.

5. Add the cauliflower, broth and red pepper. Leave to simmer for 10-20 minutes.

6. Blend the mixture in an immersion blender while ensuring that the fats are emulsified. Add the heavy cream and combine.

7. Serve with goat cheese and bacon crisps.

Storage: Keep in a covered container for 1 day or freeze for 3-4 months.

Usage: Heat in microwave or on stovetop.

Nutrition Per Serving:

Calories: 345, Fats: 32g, Protein: 6.4g, Carbs: 6.2g

Cauliflower And Shrimp Curry

A very rich curry with unique flavors.

Servings: 6

Preparation time: 15 minutes

Cooking time: 1 hour 50 minutes

Ingredients:

1/2 medium cauliflower head, cut into florets

5 cups of raw spinach

24 ounces of shrimp, deveined and detailed

4 cups of chicken stock

1 cup of unsweetened coconut milk

1/4 cup of heavy cream

1/4 cup of butter

1 medium onion, sliced into small strips

3 tablespoons of olive oil

1 tablespoon of cumin

1 tablespoon of coconut flour

2 tablespoons of curry powder

2 teaspoons of garlic powder

1 teaspoon of paprika

1 teaspoon of chili powder

1 teaspoon of cayenne

1 teaspoon of onion powder

1/2 teaspoon of coriander

1/2 teaspoon of dried and ground ginger

1/2 teaspoon of turmeric

1/2 teaspoon of pepper

1/4 teaspoon of xanthan gum, divided

1/4 teaspoon of cardamom

1/4 teaspoon of cinnamon

Salt

Pepper

Directions:

1. Heat the oil in a pan and sauté the onion until it is tender. Season with salt and pepper.

2. Add the heavy cream and 1/8 teaspoon of xanthan gum. Stir to mix.

3. Add the butter and stir.

4. Add all the spices and stir to combine. Leave to cook for 1-2 minutes.

5. Add the chicken stock and coconut milk. Bring to a boil, cover and reduce heat to low. Leave to simmer for 30-45 minutes.

6. Add the cauliflower florets to the pan and combine thoroughly. Uncover and cook for 15-20 minutes.

7. Add the shrimp and combine. Allow to cook for an extra 10-20 minutes while uncovered.

8. Mix the coconut flour and remaining xanthan gum into the pan. Leave to simmer for an additional 5-10 minutes.

9. Add the spinach and leave it to wilt. Adjust seasoning.

10. Stir the curry when the spinach wilts then cook for additional 4-5 minutes.

Storage: Store in an airtight container in the fridge for 1-2 days or freeze for 2 months.

Usage: Heat in microwave.

Nutrition Per Serving:

Calories: 331, Fats: 19.5g, Protein: 27.4g, Carbs: 5.6g

Crockpot Spicy Lime Garlic Chicken
Let your slow cooker do all the work.

Servings: 6

Preparation time: 10 minutes

Cooking time: 6 hours

Ingredients:

1 1/2 pounds of chicken thighs or breasts, boneless and skinless

1/3 cup of fresh flat leaf Italian parsley or cilantro

1/3 cup of tomato sauce

3 tablespoons of lime juice

2 tablespoons of olive or avocado oil

2 tablespoons of canned mild green chilies

2-3 garlic cloves

1 tablespoon of apple cider vinegar

1 1/2 teaspoons of sweetener (coconut sugar or swerve)

1 teaspoon of sea salt

1 teaspoon of ground chipotle powder

1/4 teaspoon of black pepper

Directions:

1. Blend all the ingredients (except chicken) in a blender or food processor until smooth.

2. Add the chicken to a crockpot, add the sauce over the chicken, cover and cook on low for 6-8 hours or 4-6 hours on high.

Storage: Store in an airtight container and refrigerate for a day or freeze for 3 months.

Usage: Heat in microwave.

Nutrition Per Serving:

Calories: 183, Fat: 9g, Protein: 22g, Carb: 2g

Pork Stew
Made with the freshest of ingredients.

Servings: 4

Preparation time: 15 minutes

Cooking time: 4 hours

Ingredients:

2 pounds of cooked pork shoulder, sliced, cut into bite-size chunks

6 ounces of button mushrooms

2 cups of chicken broth

2 cups of thick bone broth

2 bay leaves

1/2 red bell pepper, sliced

1/2 green bell pepper, sliced

1/2 jalapeno, sliced

1/2 medium onion

1 teaspoon of minced garlic

2 teaspoons of cumin

2 teaspoons of chili powder

1 teaspoon of oregano

1 teaspoon of paprika

1/4 teaspoon of cinnamon

1/2 lime, juiced

1/4 cup of tomato paste

1/2 cup of strong coffee

1/2 teaspoon of salt

1/2 teaspoon of pepper

Directions:

1. Heat 2 tablespoons of olive oil over high heat.

2. Sauté the veggies until they are fragrant and a bit cooked.

3. Add the chicken broth, bone broth and coffee to a crockpot.

4. Add in the mushrooms and pork. Stir to combine.

5. Add the veggies and spices to the crockpot, stir and cook for 4-10 hours on low.

6. Remove the lid when it is done and stir. Serve.

Storage: Freeze for up to 4 months in an airtight container or refrigerate for 2-3 days.

Usage: Heat in microwave or on stovetop.

Nutrition Per Serving:

Calories: 386, Fats: 28.9g, Protein: 19.9g, Carbs: 6.4g

Turkey Lettuce Wraps

This Thai-inspire dish makes a great lunch.

Servings: 6

Preparation time: 10 minutes

Cooking time: 15 minutes

Ingredients:

For the sauce:

3 tablespoons of soy sauce

2 tablespoons of water

2 tablespoons of rice vinegar

1 tablespoon of lime juice

1 teaspoon of sesame oil

1/4 cup of peanut butter

For the filling:

1 pound of lean ground turkey

1 cup of shredded carrots

3 garlic cloves, crushed

1 onion, chopped finely

1 tablespoon of olive oil

1 tablespoon of Thai red curry paste

For serving:

7 ounces of romaine leaf

Green onions

Peanuts

Directions:

1. Combine peanut sauce ingredients in a jar, cover with lid then shake and keep aside.

2. In a large pan, heat olive oil and sauté the garlic, onions and curry paste. Stir for 2-3 minutes until the curry paste is well heated and mixed with the onions.

3. Add the turkey and cook for 5-7 minutes while breaking it up with a spatula, until the turkey is well cooked and the color is no longer pink.

4. Add the carrots and pour the sauce over the turkey mix. Combine thoroughly and remove from heat.

5. Scoop 1/4 cup of the turkey mixture into a romaine leaf. Sprinkle with peanuts and green onions.

Storage: Portion in containers and refrigerate for up to 4 days or freeze for 2 months.

Usage: Heat in microwave.

Nutrition Per Serving:

Calories: 264, Fat: 15g, Protein: 20g, Carbs: 11g

Vegan Coconut Curry

Brighten your day with this colorful dish.

Servings: 2

Preparation time: 10 minutes

Cooking time: 20 minutes

Ingredients:

1 cup of broccoli florets

1/2 cup of coconut cream or milk

4 tablespoons of coconut oil

1 tablespoon of red curry paste

1 large handful of spinach

1/4 medium onion, chopped

2 teaspoons of soy sauce

2 teaspoons of fish sauce

1 teaspoon of minced ginger

1 teaspoon of minced garlic

Directions:

1. Heat 2 tablespoons of oil in a pan on medium-high heat.

2. Sauté the onions for 3-4 minutes until it becomes semi-translucent and caramelize.

3. Add the garlic and sauté for about 30 seconds until it is slightly brown.

4. Reduce heat to medium low and add in the broccoli. Combine thoroughly and leave for about 1-2 minutes.

5. Push the mixture to the side and add 1 tablespoon of curry paste.

6. Wait for the curry paste to start smelling strongly then stir together with the other contents of the pan. Top with the spinach.

7. Add the coconut cream or milk once the spinach starts to wilt then stir to combine.

8. Add the remaining ingredients and leave to simmer for 5-10 minutes.

Storage: Store for up to 3 days in a refrigerator or freezer for 2 weeks.

Usage: Heat in a microwave.

Nutrition Per Serving:

Calories: 393, Fat: 38.5g, Protein 5.5g, Carbs: 6.8g

Cheeseburger Salad

A healthier version of your favorite fast food salad.

Servings: 6

Preparation time: 10 minutes

Cooking time: 12 minutes

Ingredients:

For the salad:

1 pound of ground beef

8 ounces of romaine lettuce

1 cup of chopped tomatoes

1/2 cup of diced pickles

3/4 cup of shredded cheddar cheese

1/4 teaspoon of black pepper

1 teaspoon of sea salt

For the dressing:

2 tablespoons of chopped pickles

1/2 cup of mayonnaise

2 tsp mustard

1 1/2 tablespoons of powdered erythriol

1/2 teaspoon of smoked paprika

1 teaspoon of white vinegar

Directions:

1. In a pan, cook the beef over high heat. Season with salt and pepper.

2. Stir-fry the beef for about 7-10 minutes while breaking it into pieces with a spatula, until the moisture has evaporated and it turns brown.

3. Process all the dressing ingredients in a blender. Place in the fridge until you are ready to use.

4. In a large bowl, mix the salad ingredients with the beef. Toss with the dressing.

Storage: Store in an airtight container and refrigerate for up to 2 days.

Usage: Remove from fridge and eat at room temperature.

Nutrition Per Serving:

Calories: 368, Fat: 31g, Protein: 18g, Carb: 3g

DINNER

Spicy Chicken Chowder

Servings: 6

Preparation time: 10 minutes

Cooking time: 35 minutes

Ingredients:

1 1/2 pounds chicken thighs, boneless, skinless

1/2 pound bacon

6 cups of chicken stock

1/2 teaspoon garlic powder

1/2 teaspoon onion powder

Salt, to taste

Ground pepper to taste

4 chipotle peppers in Adobo sauce, minced

3 cups heavy cream

2 tablespoons fresh cilantro, to serve

Directions:

1. Add bacon to a skillet and sauté until crisp. Remove from the skillet and set aside.

2. Cut the chicken into chunks then add to the bacon grease in the skillet. Sauté until light brown on all sides.

3. Stir in the chicken stock, garlic powder, onion powder, salt, and pepper. Let simmer until the chicken is cooked through, about 13-15 minutes.

4. Stir in the chipotles and heavy cream. let simmer for additional 5 minutes.

5. Serve topped with the cooked bacon and a sprinkle of cilantro.

Storage: Keep in an airtight container in the fridge for a couple of days.

Usage: Heat up in the microwave.

Nutrition Per Serving:

Calories: 625, Fat: 42.9g, Protein: 52.4g, Carbs: 7.1g

Balsamic Chicken

A flavorful chicken meal prep with just a few ingredients.

Servings: 12

Preparation time: 30 minutes

Cooking time: 15 minutes

Ingredients:

3 pounds chicken breast

4 tablespoons balsamic vinegar

1 tablespoon red chili sauce

1 tablespoon honey

1 teaspoon ginger

Directions:

1. Preheat the oven to 405F.

2. Combine balsamic vinegar, red chili sauce, honey and ginger in a small bowl. Mix well.

3. Add the chicken to a Ziploc bag then add the balsamic mixture. Shake to coat then set aside to

marinate for 30 minutes.

4. Transfer chicken pieces to a sheet pan. Bake for about 15 minutes.

Storage: Can be kept in the fridge for 4 days. Will keep for up to 2 months in the freezer.

Usage: Heat up in the microwave.

Nutrition Per Serving:

Calories: 132, Fat: 2g, Protein: 26g, Carbs: 3g

Keto Goulash

This low carb goulash combines tender cauliflower, tomato and beef wonderfully.

Servings: 5

Preparation time: 5 minutes

Cooking time: 20 minutes

Ingredients:

1 1/2 pounds of lean ground beef

Salt and pepper

1/2 small onion, chopped

1/2 bell pepper, diced

1 medium head cauliflower broken into florets

1 (14 ounce) can diced tomatoes drained, juice reserved

2 cups of water

1 tablespoon of tomato paste

1/4 teaspoon garlic powder, optional

Directions:

1. Add ground beef to a heavy skillet and cook until browned.

2. Add onion and bell pepper. Cook and stir until the veggies are tender.

3. Stir in cauliflower, reserved tomato juice and water.

4. Bring to a gentle boil then cover and let simmer until the cauliflower is tender, about 5 minutes.

5. If there is still too much liquid, uncover and allow to simmer until the liquid has reduced.

6. Stir in the tomatoes, tomato paste and garlic powder. Serve.

Storage: Cool in the fridge then freeze in sealable containers.

Usage: Heat up in the microwave.

Nutrition Per Serving:

Calories: 191, Fat: 5g, Protein: 30g, Carbs: 8g

Simple Beef Stew

Has a deep tantalizing flavor.

Servings: 6

Preparation time: 20 minutes

Cooking time: 2 hours

Ingredients:

4 cups of beef broth

2 pounds of beef stew meat

2 tablespoons of garlic, crushed

4 medium celery sticks, cut into 1-inch slices

3 medium carrots, cut into 1-inch slices

1 small yellow onion, diced

1 1/2 teaspoons of salt

1 teaspoon of paprika

1 teaspoon of pepper

1 teaspoon of Worcestershire

Directions:

1. Season the meat with salt and pepper.

2. In a large pot, brown the beef in oil over medium heat.

3. Add in the paprika, beef broth, garlic, Worcestershire, onions and stir. Leave to boil then turn down the heat to low medium. Cover and allow to simmer for 90 minutes.

4. Add the celery and carrots. Cover and allow to simmer for an extra 30-45 minutes or until the veggies are soft.

Storage: Keep in an airtight container and refrigerate for 1 day or freeze for up to 4-6 months.

Usage: Heat in microwave or stovetop

Nutrition Per Serving:

Calories: 292, Protein: 28.7g, Fat: 16.2g, Carb: 4g

Bacon Topped Meatloaf
A yummy recipe that is totally low carb.

Servings: 12

Preparation time: 15 minutes

Cooking time: 50 minutes

Ingredients:

1.6 pounds of ground beef

1.6 pounds of ground pork

8 bacon slices

2 garlic cloves

2 eggs

1 spring onion

2 tablespoons of sundried tomatoes

2 teaspoons of dried oregano

A handful of fresh basil

A handful of fresh parsley

Salt

Pepper

1 cup of grated parmesan cheese, optional

Directions:

1. Grease and line a baking dish.

2. Mix all the ingredients in a large bowl with your hands until well mixed.

3. Shape into a large meatloaf on the baking dish.

4. Cover the meatloaf with the bacon slices and sprinkle with parmesan cheese if using.

5. Bake for 50 minutes at 350F or until it is well cooked in the centre.

Storage: Freeze in an airtight container for 2-3 months.

Usage: Heat in microwave.

Nutrition Per Serving:

Calories: 370, Fat: 25g, Protein: 35g, Carb: 1.2g

Cheddar Cheese Broccoli Soup
A creamy bowl of comfort.

Servings: 4

Preparation time: 5 minutes

Cooking time: 22 minutes

Ingredients:

4 cups of chopped broccoli

3 cups of sharp cheddar cheese, shredded

3/4 cup of heavy cream

1 1/2 cups of vegetable stock

1 small onion, chopped

1 teaspoon of minced garlic

Salt

Pepper

Directions:

1. Combine the veggie stock, broccoli, onions and garlic in a large saucepan. Cook for about 5 minutes over medium heat.

2. Bring to a low boil, cover and allow to simmer for 10 minutes.

3. Add the heavy cream, stir and cook for 3-5 minutes.

4. Add the cheese and cook for about 1-2 minutes until smooth.

5. Season with salt and pepper

Storage: Keep in an airtight container and refrigerate for 1 day or freeze for up to 6 months.

Usage: Heat in microwave or stovetop.

Nutrition Per Serving:

Calories: 561, Fat: 52.3g, Protein: 23.9g, Carbs: 9.9g

Spicy Chili Soup

Cuddle up with a bowl of this delicious soup on cold nights.

Servings: 4

Preparation time: 10 minutes

Cooking time: 40 minutes

Ingredients:

1 pound of chicken thighs

2 ounces of queso fresco

2 cups of water

2 cups of chicken broth

4 tablespoons of fresh cilantro, chopped

4 tablespoons of tomato paste

1 medium avocado

2 medium chili peppers, sliced

1/2 lime, juiced

2 tablespoons of olive oil

2 tablespoons of butter

1 teaspoon of turmeric

1 teaspoon of coriander seeds

1/2 teaspoon of ground cumin

Salt

Pepper

Directions:

1. Cut the chicken and cook in an oiled skillet. Season with salt and pepper and keep aside.

2. Heat the coriander seeds in 2 tablespoon of oil to release their flavor. When the coriander seeds become fragrant, stir in the chili peppers.

3. Add the water and broth and leave to simmer. Season with the salt, turmeric, pepper and cumin.

4. Add the butter and tomato paste once the soup begins to simmer. Stir to mix. Leave to simmer for about 5-10 minutes.

5. Turn down the heat and add the lime juice.

6. Put 4 ounces of chicken in each serving bowl then ladle the soup over it.

7. Garnish with 1/2 ounce of queso fresco, 1/4 avocado and cilantro.

Storage: Freeze in a freezer bag or airtight container for up to 6 months.

Usage: Heat on stovetop or microwave.

Nutrition Per Serving:

Calories: 369.5, Fats: 25.8g, Protein: 27g, Carbs: 6.5g

Lasagna With Zoodles
The classic comfort food.

Servings: 4

Preparation time: 10 minutes

Cooking time: 40 minutes

Ingredients:

1 pound ground beef

10 ounces of ricotta cheese

4 ounces of shredded mozzarella cheese

1 cup of marinara

1 large zucchini, sliced into strips

Directions:

1. Preheat oven to 350F.

2. Salt the zucchini strips and allow to stand for 15 minutes.

3. In a pan, brown the beef and add the marinara. Add salt and pepper to generously.

4. In a small casserole dish, layer the meat, followed by zucchini, ricotta, then the meat, zucchini, another ricotta and then mozzarella.

5. Cover the dish with foil then bake for 30 minutes.

6. Uncover and broil for 2 or 3 minutes until the top is browned.

Storage: Keep in an airtight container and refrigerate for 3-5 days or freeze for 2-3 months.

Usage: Heat in microwave.

Nutrition Per Serving:

Calories: 573, Fat: 46g, Protein: 33g, Carbs: 5g

Kale Sausage Soup
This dish is always a winner.

Servings: 6

Preparation time: 15 minutes

Cooking time: 25 minutes

Ingredients:

1 pound of sweet Italian ground sausage

4 cups of reduced sodium chicken broth

3 cups of chopped kale

1 cup of heavy whipped cream

2 garlic cloves, minced

1 medium carrot, peeled and chopped

1 medium yellow onion, diced

1/2 medium head cauliflower, cut into small florets

2 tablespoons of red wine vinegar

1 tablespoon of butter

1 teaspoon of dried rubbed stage

1 teaspoon of dried oregano

1 teaspoon of dried basil

Sea salt, to taste

1/2 teaspoon of freshly ground black pepper

1/4 -1/2 teaspoon of crushed red pepper flakes

Directions:

1. Over medium high, heat a large pan and add the sausage, using a large spoon to break it up. Cook for about 5 minutes until well cooked and browned. Stir occasionally.

2. Remove the sausage with a slotted spoon to a plate lined with paper towels. Allow to drain.

3. Discard the drippings from the pan. Add the butter and melt over medium heat. Sauté the onion and carrot, until the onion starts to brown at the edges and becomes a bit translucent.

4. Add the garlic, stir and cook for 1 minute.

5. Pour in the vinegar and cook until it becomes like syrup, using a spoon to scrape up browned bits.

6. Stir in the basil, pepper flakes, oregano and sage. Add the heavy cream and stock. Turn up the heat to medium high.

7. Add the cauliflower when the soup begins to simmer then reduce the heat to medium low. Uncover and simmer for about 10 minutes or until the cauliflower is soft enough to be pierced easily with a fork.

8. Stir in the sausage and kale. Cook for an additional 1-2 minutes or until the sausage is reheated and the kale wilts.

9. Season with salt and pepper.

Storage: Store in an airtight container or freezer bag and refrigerate for 2 days or freeze for 2-3 months.

Usage: Heat in microwave.

Nutrition Per Serving:

Calories: 298, Fats: 24g, Protein: 16g, Carbs: 6g

Spicy Pumpkin Soup
Simple, satisfying and tasty.

Servings: 3

Preparation time: 15 minutes

Cooking time: 50 minutes

Ingredients:

4 bacon slices

1 1/2 cups of chicken broth

1 cup of pumpkin puree

1/2 cup of heavy cream

2 roasted garlic cloves, crushed

1 bay leaf

1/4 medium onion, diced

4 tablespoons of butter

3 tablespoons of bacon grease (from cooking the bacon)

1/2 teaspoon of fresh ginger, minced

1/2 teaspoon of salt

1/2 teaspoon of pepper

1/4 teaspoon of coriander

1/4 teaspoon of cinnamon

1/8 teaspoon of nutmeg

2 tablespoons of sour cream, optional

Grated parmesan cheese, optional

Directions:

1. Melt the butter in a large pan over medium low heat.

2. Mix all the spices together in a small bowl.

3. Sauté the ginger, onion and garlic in the pan for about 2-3 minutes or until the onions begin to turn translucent.

4. Add the spices and cook for 1-2 minutes.

5. Add the pumpkin puree and stir everything together.

6. Add the broth and stir to combine. Allow to boil, reduce heat to low and allow to simmer for 20 minutes.

7. Blend in an immersion blender until it forms a smooth puree. Return to pot and cook for an extra 20 minutes.

8. Meanwhile, cook the bacon slices over medium heat.

9. Pour in the heavy cream and bacon grease into the soup once it is done. Stir to combine.

10. Crumble the bacon over the soup. Serve with parsley and sour cream if desired.

Storage: Freeze in a covered container for up to 2-3 months.

Usage: Heat in microwave or on stove top.

Nutrition Per Serving:

Calories: 486, Fats: 48.7g, Protein: 5.7g, Carbs: 7.3g

Crockpot Butter Chicken
Absolutely drool-worthy

Servings: 4-6

Preparation time: 10 minutes

Cooking time: 8 hours

Ingredients:

1 (14-ounce) can of full fat coconut milk

1 (6-ounce) can of tomato paste

1 pound of chicken thighs or breast, boneless and skinless

1/4 cup of cilantro

4 garlic cloves, minced finely

1 medium onion, chopped

2 teaspoons of coconut oil

1 teaspoon of cumin

1 teaspoon of coriander

1 teaspoon of fresh ginger, minced finely

1 teaspoon of cardamom

Juice of 1 lime

1/2 teaspoon of salt

1/4 - 1/2 teaspoon of cayenne pepper, optional

Directions:

1. Heat oil in a medium pan and sauté the onion until it is slightly soft and translucent.

2. Add the spices, garlic, salt and ginger. Cook for an additional minute until the spices are fragrant. Add the milk and tomato paste. Stir to mix well.

3. Add the chicken to the crockpot and pour the sauce over it.

4. Cook for 6-8 hours on low or 3-4 hours on high.

5. Shred the chicken and add to the sauce with the lime juice. Top with cilantro and serve.

Storage: Refrigerate in airtight container for up to 2 days or freeze for 5-6 months.

Usage: Heat in microwave.

Nutrition Per Serving:

Calories: 472, Protein: 14.0g, Fat: 7.4g, Carbs: 3.2g

Crockpot Beef Curry

A dish made with a Malaysian twist.

Servings: 6

Preparation time: 10 minutes

Cooking time: 8 hours

Ingredients:

1.8 pound of beef, cut into large pieces

1 cup of coconut cream

4 whole cloves

1 red onion, quartered

2 teaspoons of cilantro or coriander

1 teaspoon of turmeric

1 teaspoon of ground cardamom

1 teaspoon of ground cumin

1 teaspoon of ground cinnamon

1 teaspoon of Chinese five spice

A large handful of leafy greens

1/2 teaspoon of chili powder

Directions:

1. Put the spices and coconut cream in a crockpot.

2. Add the beef and onion, combine.

3. Cook for 8-10 hours on low or 4-6 hours on high.

4. About 5 minutes before serving, add the greens to the crockpot and gently fold them in.

Storage: Keep in an airtight container and refrigerate for 1-2 days or freeze for 2-3 months.

Usage: Heat in microwave.

Nutrition Per Serving:

Calories: 256, Fat: 14.1g, Protein: 29.1g, Carb: 2g

Vegetable Soup
A delicious and colorful way to keep warm on a chilly night.

Servings: 14

Preparation time: 14 minutes

Cooking time: 18 minutes

Ingredients:

1 (28-ounce) can of reduced sodium diced tomatoes

6 cups of reduced sodium beef broth

4 cups of chopped cabbage

2 cups of sliced zucchini

2 cups of broccoli florets

1 cup of green beans, cut into 1-inch pieces

1 cup of chopped carrots

2 garlic cloves, crushed

2 bell peppers, diced

2 bay leaves

1 small onion, chopped

2 tablespoons of tomato paste

Pepper

1/2 teaspoon of basil

1/2 teaspoon of thyme

Directions:

1. Cook the garlic and onion in a large pot over medium heat until onion softens slightly.

2. Add the cabbage, carrots and green beans. Cook for an extra 5 minutes.

3. Add the tomatoes with its juice, bell peppers, bay leaves, broth, seasonings and tomato paste. Allow to simmer for 6-7 minutes.

4. Add the broccoli and zucchini. Simmer for an extra 5 minutes or until the veggies soften.

5. Remove bay leaves and serve.

Storage: Freeze in a covered container for up to 4 months.

Usage: Heat in microwave.

Nutrition Per Serving:

Calories: 98, Fat: 2.7g, Protein: 5.8g, Carb: 4.6g

Crockpot Beef Stew
Easy, comforting and yummy.

Servings: 6

Preparation time: 15 minutes

Cooking time: 6 hours

Ingredients:

2 1/2 pounds of beef chuck roast, boneless, cut into 1-inch cubes

2 cups of sliced mushrooms

1 cup of beef broth

1/2 cup of red wine

1/3 cup of fresh Italian parsley, crushed

3 tablespoons of tomato paste

3 carrots, diced

3 garlic cloves, minced

2 bay leaves

1 yellow onion, chopped

1 pinch of red pepper flakes

1 teaspoon of dried thyme

1 teaspoon of dried rosemary

1 teaspoon of salt

1 teaspoon of black pepper

Directions:

1. Season the roast with salt and pepper. Put in a crockpot.

2. Whisk together the broth with tomato paste in a small bowl. Pour over the roast along with the red wine.

3. Add the remaining ingredients except the parsley. Stir to combine.

4. Cover and cook for 4-6 hours on low or for 2-3 hours on high until the veggies are soft and the meat is well cooked.

5. Remove bay leaves, garnish with parsley and serve.

Storage: Freeze in covered container for up to 6 months.

Usage: Heat in microwave or stovetop.

Nutrition Per Serving:

Calories: 362, Fat: 14.5g, Protein: 52g, Carbs: 7.0g,

Parmesan Coated Pork Chops

A quick dinner to for busy nights.

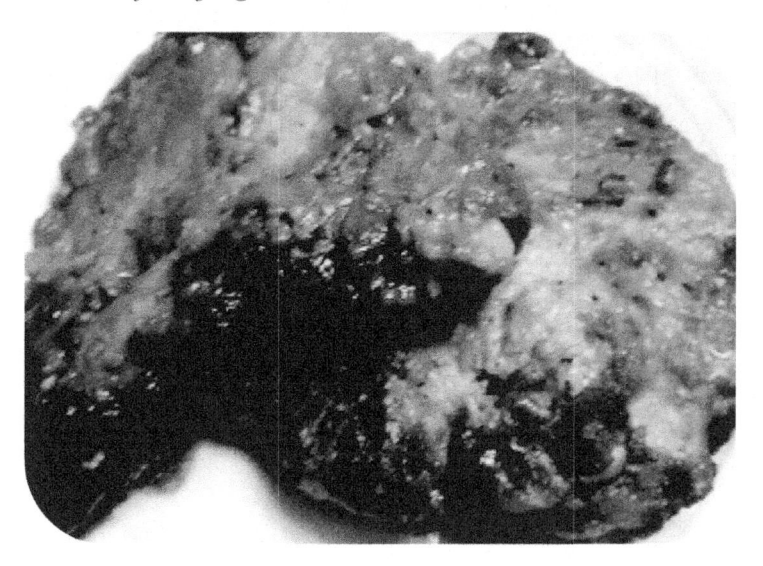

Servings: 14

Preparation time: 10 minutes

Cooking time: 12 minutes

Ingredients:

14 bone-in pork chops

6 ounces of parmesan cheese, grated

3/4 cup of almond flour

2 large eggs

Salt

Pepper

Directions:

1. Mix the cheese with the almond flour, salt and pepper.

2. Beat the eggs and keep in a shallow dish.

3. Dip the pork in the eggs and dredge in the cheese mixture.

4. In a pan, fry the chops in bacon grease for 1 minute on each side.

5. Cook in the oven for about 10 minutes at 400F.

Storage: Keep in an airtight container and refrigerate for 3-4 days or freeze for 2-3 months.

Usage: Heat in microwave.

Nutrition Per Serving:

Calories: 454, Fat: 34g, Protein: 33g, Carbs: 4g

SNACKS

Coconut And Almond Bark
All of the sweetness made with no sugar.

Servings: 12

Preparation time: 15 minutes

Cooking time: 10 minutes

Ingredients:

1 cup of dark chocolate

1/2 cup of unsweetened coconut flakes

1/2 cup of almonds

1/2 cup of coconut butter

10 drops of liquid stevia, optional

1/2 teaspoon of almond extract, optional

1/4 teaspoon of sea salt

Directions:

1. Preheat oven to 350F.

2. Line a baking sheet with foil and spread the coconut and almonds on it.

3. Toast in the oven for 5-8 minutes. Stir once or twice to prevent from burning. When everything is evenly toasted, remove from the oven and keep aside to cool.

4. Melt the chocolate in a double boiler and add the butter once it has slightly melted. Add the almond extract and stevia if using. Stir thoroughly to combine and keep aside.

5. Pour the mixture into a baking sheet lined with wax or parchment paper. Use a spatula or the back of a spoon to evenly spread it out.

6. Scatter the toasted coconut flakes and almond mix over the top and use your hands to gently press so that it touches the chocolate.

7. Lightly sprinkle salt over it and refrigerate for an hour at least to set it.

8. Slice with a pizza roller or knife once it has set.

Storage: Keep in an airtight container.

Usage: Enjoy any time.

Nutrition Per Serving:

Calories: 173, Fat: 16g, Protein: 3g, Carbs: 3.5g

Pecan Butter Ice Cream

Everyone in your home will love this.

Servings: 6

Preparation time: 10 minutes

Cooking time: 5 minutes

Ingredients:

1 cup of heavy cream

2/3 cup of pecans, chopped

2 egg yolks

1 pinch of stevia

1/3 cup of erythritol

2 tablespoons of butter

1 teaspoon of vanilla extract

1/8 teaspoon of xanthan gum

Directions:

1. In a pan, melt the butter on a low heat until it is slightly brown. Add the heavy cream and bring it to a simmer.

2. Reduce heat to its lowest and add the erythriol. Allow it to completely dissolve while gently stirring. Transfer to a mixing bowl and add the stevia. Mix all the ingredients with an electric hand mixer at medium speed.

3. Add the xanthan gum while still mixing.

4. Separate the egg yolks in a small bowl and add the vanilla extract. Whisk slowly and add to the mixing bowl while the mixing is still running.

5. Add the pecans and use a spoon to fold them in.

6. Freeze the bowl for about 3 hours or until you can easily scoop it.

Storage: Freeze in an airtight container for up to 3 months.

Usage: Thaw it a bit in the refrigerator before serving.

Nutrition Per Serving:

Calories: 200, Fat: 20g, Protein: 2g, Carbs: 1g

Creamy Cranberry Muffins

A fluffy snack ideal for cranberry season.

Servings: 12

Preparation time: 10 minutes

Cooking time: 30 minutes

Ingredients:

3 cups of almond flour

1 cup of cranberries

1/2 cup of sour cream

1/2 cup of swerve sweetener

1/2 cup of chopped pecans, optional

4 large eggs

2 teaspoons of baking powder

1 teaspoon of vanilla extract

1/2 teaspoon of cinnamon

1/4 teaspoon of salt

Directions:

1. Preheat oven to 325F.

2. Line a muffin pan with silicone or parchment paper.

3. Blend the eggs, sour cream and vanilla extract in a blender for about 30 seconds.

4. Add the baking powder, almond flour, sweetener, salt and cinnamon. Blend for about 30 seconds to 1 minute, until smooth.

5. Stir in the cranberries and pecans with your hand. Reserve a few of the cranberries for toppings.

6. Evenly divide the batter among the muffin cups and bake for 25-30 minutes until it firm and golden brown.

Storage: Store in an airtight container and refrigerate for a week or freeze for 3-4 months.

Usage: Heat in microwave.

Nutrition Per Serving:

Calories: 241, Fat: 20.24g, Protein: 8.75g, Carbs: 8.4g

Chia Almond Butter Squares

A healthy and great tasting fat bomb recipe.

Servings: 14

Preparation time: 10 minutes

Cooking time: 5 minutes

Ingredients:

1/2 cup of coconut cream, melted

1/2 cup of raw almonds, toasted

1/2 cup of unsweetened coconut flakes, shredded

1/4 cup of chia seeds, ground

1/4 cup of heavy whipping cream

4 tablespoons of erythriol

2 tablespoons of butter

2 tablespoons of coconut flour

4 teaspoons of coconut oil

1 1/2 teaspoons of vanilla extract

1/4 teaspoon of liquid stevia

Directions:

1. Grind the almonds in a food processor until you get a mealy substance. Add 2 tablespoons of erythriol and a teaspoon of coconut oil. Mix until it forms almond butter.

2. In a pan, heat the butter until it is browned. Add the heavy cream, vanilla, stevia and remaining erythriol. Combine until it forms a bubbly mixture. Add the almond butter and combine.

3. In a pan, toast the ground chia seeds and coconut flakes for some minutes.

4. Mix everything together and add the coconut flour, coconut cream and remaining coconut oil. Combine thoroughly and scoop into a square dish.

5. Keep in refrigerator for an hour at least. Divide into small squares and refrigerate for some hours.

Storage: Refrigerate in an airtight container.

Usage: Eat at any time.

Nutrition Per Serving:

Calories: 145.7, Fats: 13.6g, Protein: 2.8g, Carbs: 1.9g

Beef Jerky

Enjoy this snack whenever and wherever.

Servings: 8

Preparation time: 15 minutes

Cooking time: 6 hours

Ingredients:

1 large London broil, fat trimmed, sliced into thin strips across the grain

1/2 cup of apple juice

2 tablespoons of kosher salt

1 tablespoon of red pepper flakes

1 1/2 teaspoon of garlic powder

1 teaspoon of ground coriander

1 teaspoon of black pepper

1 teaspoon of ground allspice

1 teaspoon of lime juice

Directions:

1. Mix all the ingredients except the meat in a large bowl or bag. Add the beef strips and toss to coat. Refrigerate for at least 8 hours or overnight.

2. Preheat oven to 250F.

3. Spread the strips on cookies sheets. Put in the oven and dry for about 6 hours until they are completely dried and dark in color.

Storage: Store in an airtight container and refrigerate.

Usage: Eat at any time.

Nutrition Per Serving:

Calories: 143, Fat: 4g, Protein: 22g, Carbs: 2.3

Cheese Chips

A delicious substitute for potato chips.

Servings: 4

Preparation time: 5 minutes

Cooking time: 10 minutes

Ingredients:

1/2 pounds of edam, provolone or cheddar cheese, cut into slices

1/2 teaspoon of paprika powder

Directions:

1. Preheat oven to 400F.

2. Line a baking sheet with parchment paper and place the slices of cheese on it. Sprinkle the paprika on top.

3. Bake for 8-10 minutes. Check frequently towards the end of the baking time to ensure that it does not burn.

Storage: Store in an airtight container in the pantry or refrigerator.

Usage: Eat at any time.

Nutrition Per Serving:

Calories: 100, Fats: 5g, Protein: 7.6g, Carbs: 6g

Low Carb Chocolate Green Smoothie

A delicious combination of healthy vegetables.

Servings: 2

Preparation time: 5 minutes

Cooking time: 0 minutes

Ingredients:

3 1/2 ounces of chopped spinach

1 cup of coconut cream

1/2 cup of frozen berries

1/4 cup of cocoa powder

1 tablespoon of granulated sweetener

Directions:

1. Blend all the ingredients together until smooth.

Storage: Keep in an airtight glass jar and refrigerate for 1-2 days.

Usage: Enjoy any time.

Nutrition Per Serving:

Calories: 186, Fat: 16.3g, Protein: 4.6g, Carbs: 11.8g

Creamy Coconut Yogurt
A guilt-free snack with no extra calories.

Servings: 4

Preparation time: 15 minutes

Cooking time: 0 minutes

Ingredients:

1 can of full fat coconut milk

2/3 cup of heavy whipping cream

2 capsules of probiotic-10

1/2 teaspoon of xanthan gum

Your desired toppings

Directions:

1. Thoroughly stir the can of milk and pour into a container.

2. Add the content of the capsules to the container. Place the container in the oven with the light of the oven on for 12-24 hours.

3. Remove from oven and pour it into a mixing bowl or place in refrigerator to cool.

4. Add the xanthan gum and mix with a hand blender.

5. Whip the cream in another bowl until it forms stiff peaks.

6. Add the cream to the yogurt and mix on low speed until it achieves the desired consistency.

Storage: Freeze in an airtight container.

Usage: Enjoy any time.

Nutrition Per Serving:

Calories: 315, Fats: 31.3g, Protein: 0g, Carbs: 4.3g

Coconut And Chocolate Fat Bombs
So delicious and so easy.

Servings: 14

Preparation time: 15 minutes

Cooking time: 0 minutes

Ingredients:

4 ounces of raw dark chocolate chips

2 cups of unsweetened shredded coconut

1/3 cup of melted coconut oil

2 tablespoons of raw honey

1/2 teaspoon of vanilla bean powder, optional

Directions:

1. Blend all the ingredients apart from the chocolate chips in a blender until crumbly and fine.

2. Prepare a baking sheet by lining it with wax paper. Using a tablespoon measuring spoon, scoop the mixture and use your hands to form into small mounds. Set the mounds onto the wax paper. Keep in freezer to set for about 10 minutes.

3. Melt the chocolate in a double boiler until smooth. Drizzle the bombs with chocolate, using a butter knife.

4. Return to the fridge for 10 minutes to allow it set.

Storage: Store in refrigerator for a week.

Usage: Enjoy any time.

Nutrition Per Serving:

Calories: 108, Fat: 8.7g, Protein: 0.9g, Carbs: 7.5g

Kale Chips
Crunchy and satisfying.

Servings: 4

Preparation time: 5 minutes

Cooking time: 12 minutes

Ingredients:

1 large bunch of kale

2 tablespoons of olive oil

1 tablespoon of seasoned salt

Directions:

1. Preheat oven to 350F.

2. Discard the kale stems, wash and dry well.

3. Put the kale in a Ziploc bag with the oil and shake thoroughly to coat.

4. Spread the kale on a baking sheet then flatten the leaves. Bake for 12 minutes, remove and season with salt.

Storage: Store in an airtight container and keep refrigerated.

Usage: Eat at any time.

Nutrition Per Serving:

Calories: 80.5, Fats: 7.2g, Protein: 1.8g, Carbs: 1.3g,

Green Beans Fries

Enjoy with your favorite dip.

Servings: 4

Preparation time: 10 minutes

Cooking time: 10 minutes

Ingredients:

12 ounces of green beans, fibrous end cut off

2/3 cup of grated parmesan

1 large egg

1/2 teaspoon of pink Himalayan salt

1/2 teaspoon of garlic powder, optional

1/4 teaspoon of black pepper

1/4 teaspoon of paprika, optional

Directions:

1. Preheat oven to 400F.

2. In a shallow dish, mix the parmesan with the seasonings.

3. In a large bowl, whisk the egg and coat the green beans in the mixture. Let the excess drip away for some seconds.

4. Dredge the beans in the parmesan mixture and sprinkle the cheese over it. Gently toss with hands.

5. Place the green beans on a greased baking sheet and bake for about 10 minutes until the cheese becomes slightly golden.

Storage: Store in an airtight container and keep refrigerated.

Usage: Serve with mayo or ranch.

Nutrition Per Serving:

Calories: 113, Fat: 6g, Protein: 9g, Carbs: 2.5g

Avocado Brownies
Moist, soft and yummy.

Servings: 12

Preparation time: 10 minutes

Cooking time: 35 minutes

Ingredients:

1 cup of dark chocolate

2 eggs

2 avocados, peeled

4 tablespoons of cocoa powder

3 tablespoons of refined coconut oil

1 teaspoon of stevia powder

1/2 teaspoon of vanilla

For the dry ingredients:

3/4 cup blanched almond flour

1/4 cup of erythriol

1 teaspoon of baking powder

1/4 teaspoon baking soda

1/4 teaspoon of salt

Directions:

1. Preheat oven to 350F.

2. Process the avocados in a food processor until smooth.

3. Add the vanilla, stevia, cocoa powder, coconut oil, eggs and chocolate one at a time and process for a few seconds.

4. Mix all the dry ingredients in another bowl. Add to the food processor and pulse until it is mixed.

5. Set a parchment paper piece over a baking dish and pour the batter into it. Evenly spread out the mixture with a spoon and bake for 35 minutes.

6. Remove from oven, allow to cool and cut into 12 slices.

Storage: Will keep in refrigerator for 4 days.

Usage: Eat at any time.

Nutrition Per Serving:

Calories: 158, Fat: 14.3g, Protein: 3.8g, Carbs: 9g

Sunshine Smoothie

All the flavors of summer in one place.

Servings: 1

Preparation time: 5 minutes

Cooking time: 0 minutes

Ingredients:

20 drops of liquid stevia

7 ice cubes

3/4 cup of unsweetened coconut milk

1/4 cup of sour cream

2 tablespoons of flaxseed meal

1 tablespoon of MCT oil

1/2 teaspoon of mango extract

1/4 teaspoon of banana extract

1/4 teaspoon of blueberry extract

Directions:

1. Blend all the ingredients in a blender until smooth.

2. Set aside for several minutes for the flax meal to soak up some of the liquid.

Storage: Keep refrigerated in an airtight jar for 1-2 days.

Usage: Drink any time.

Nutrition Per Serving:

Calories: 352, Fats: 31g, Protein: 5g, Carbs: 3g

Pesto Crackers
You can crunch on these all day.

Servings: 6

Preparation time: 10 minutes

Cooking time: 17 minutes

Ingredients:

1 1/4 cups of almond flour

3 tablespoons of butter

2 tablespoons of basil pesto

1 garlic clove, crushed

1/2 teaspoon of baking powder

1/2 teaspoon of salt

A pinch of cayenne pepper

1/4 teaspoon of ground black pepper

1/4 teaspoon of dried basil

Directions:

1. Preheat oven to 325F.

2. Use parchment paper to line a cookie sheet.

3. Mix the almond flour, baking powder, salt and pepper in a medium bowl until smooth.

4. Add the cayenne, basil and garlic. Stir to mix well.

5. Add the pesto and mix until the batter forms rough crumbs.

6. Using your hands or fork, cut the butter into the mixture until it forms a ball.

7. Put the batter on the cookie sheet and thinly spread it out until it is about 1/16 inch thick.

8. Bake for 15-17 minutes until it turns light golden brown.

9. Remove from oven and cut into your desired pieces.

Storage: Keep in an airtight container.

Usage: Enjoy any time.

Nutrition Per Serving:

Calories: 210, Fats: 20g, Protein: 5g, Carbs: 3g

No-Sugar Cheese Parfait With Berries
Super easy to make.

Servings: 2

Preparation time: 5 minutes

Cooking time: 0 minutes

Ingredients:

8 ounces of low fat cottage cheese

8 drops of liquid stevia

1/4 teaspoon of vanilla extract

1/8 teaspoon of cinnamon

1 cup of berries, for topping

Directions:

1. Blend all the ingredients in a blender or food processor until smooth. Top with the berries.

Storage: Keeps well in the refrigerator for a few days.

Usage: Eat at any time.

Nutrition Per Serving:

Calories: 125, Fat: 2.2g, Protein: 14.8g, Carbs: 2.5g

Pepperoni Chips

A suitable snack for movie nights.

Servings: 3-5

Preparation time: 2 minutes

Cooking time: 1 minute

Ingredients:

1 package of pepperonis

Directions:

1. Place the pepperonis on two layers of paper towels and cover with another paper towel.

2. Microwave the pepperonis for 1 minute until they are crisp and stiff.

Storage: Store in an airtight container and keep refrigerated.

Usage: Serve with salsa or any low carb dip .

Nutrition Per Serving:

Calories: 80, Fat: 4g, Protein: 9g, Carbs: 0g

Keto Queso Fresco

A recipe with zero carbs.

Servings: 5

Preparation time: 5 minutes

Cooking time: 10 minutes

Ingredients:

1 pound of queso fresco, cut into thin rectangles or cubes

1/2 tablespoon of olive oil

1 tablespoon of coconut oil

Directions:

1. In a pan, heat the olive and coconut oil over high heat.

2. Wait for the oil to hit the smoke point then add the cheese. Allow to brown on one side, then flip and brown the other side.

3. Drain the cheese on paper towels.

Storage: Keep refrigerated in an airtight container for up to 1 week.

Usage: Eat at any time.

Nutrition Per Serving:

Calories: 243, Fats: 19.5g, Protein: 16g, Carbs: 0g

Spinach Cucumber Smoothie

A refreshing green snack.

Servings: 1

Preparation time: 2 minutes

Cooking time: 0 minutes

Ingredients:

2.5 ounces of cucumber, peeled and cut into cubes

2 handfuls of spinach

1 cup of coconut milk

12 drops of liquid stevia

7 ice cubes

1-2 tablespoons of MCT oil

1/4 teaspoon of xanthan gum

Directions:

1. Blend all the ingredients in a blender until smooth.

Storage: Keep refrigerated in a covered container for 2 days.

Usage: Drink at any time.

Nutrition Per Serving:

Calories: 217, Fats: 20g, Protein: 9g, Carbs: 6g

END

Made in the USA
Coppell, TX
07 June 2021